CW01476913

Let's Discuss
POLLUTION

Mark Lambert

Wayland

Let's Discuss

Let's Discuss AIDS
Let's Discuss Animal Rights
Let's Discuss Drinking
Let's Discuss Drugs
Let's Discuss Education
Let's Discuss Family Life
Let's Discuss Health and Fitness
Let's Discuss Homelessness
Let's Discuss Law and Order
Let's Discuss the Media
Let's Discuss Old Age

Let's Discuss Pollution
Let's Discuss Pop Music
Let's Discuss Poverty
Let's Discuss Racism
Let's Discuss Religion
Let's Discuss Sex
Let's Discuss Smoking
Let's Discuss Unemployment
Let's Discuss Violence
Let's Discuss Women's Rights

First published in 1988 by
Wayland (Publishers) Ltd
61 Western Road, Hove
East Sussex BN3 1JD, England

Editor: William Wharfe
Designers: Ross George/David Armitage

**British Library Cataloguing in
Publication Data**
Lambert, Mark, 1946–
  Let's discuss pollution. — (Let's discuss)
  1. Pollution
  I. Title
  363.7'3   TD174

ISBN 1–85210–110–5

© Copyright 1988
Wayland (Publishers) Ltd

Typeset, printed and bound
in the UK at
The Bath Press, Avon

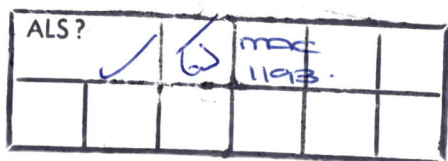

Front cover: *Modern industrial society produces huge amounts of waste: what should be done with it?*

Contents

Introduction   4
Air Pollution   7
Case Study 1: Dietrich, aged 32   13
Industrial Pollution   15
Case Study 2: Liz, aged 24   20
Farming and Pollution   22
Case Study 3: Brian, aged 48   27
Water Pollution   29
Radioactivity   34
Case Study 4: Malcolm, aged 46   40
Pollution and Society   42
Glossary   46
Further Reading   47
Index   48

The case studies in this book are fictitious. They are not subject to copyright and may be reproduced for use in the classroom

Introduction

Pollution is the contamination of the environment with poisonous or harmful substances, which are usually the result of some human activity. Just thirty years ago, pollution was regarded by most people as merely undesirable, something that made our surroundings a bit less healthy. Today, however, we know that the environment is actually being damaged by a whole range of pollutants. Many environmentalists now see pollution as one of the foremost threats to life on this planet.

Pollutants are usually waste materials, such as exhaust gases produced by cars, unwanted by-products of industrial processes, domestic rubbish and sewage. Pollution may also result from the accidental release of a chemical into the environment. Minor leaks occur every day, and sometimes there are major accidents that have catastrophic results, such as the events at Bhopal, in India, in 1984 and Chernobyl, in the USSR, in 1986. But we also

When methyl isocyanate gas was accidentally released at Bhopal in India, many people suffered damage to their eyes and lungs. Over 2000 died.

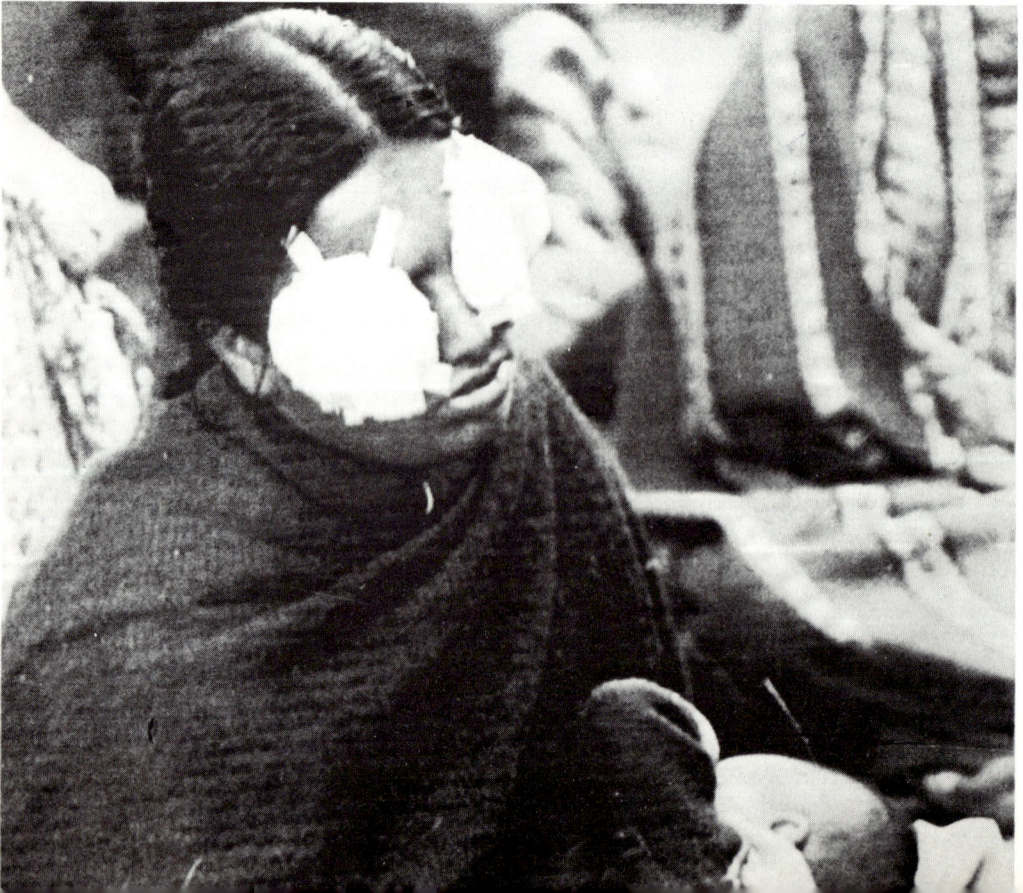

During the 1950s smog was a regular occurrence in London. People were asked not to stoke up their coal fires unduly.

deliberately release a number of chemicals into the environment for specific reasons. For instance, crops are sprayed with chemical pesticides, some of which are truly man-made pollutants—chemicals that do not occur in nature and cannot be broken down by any natural processes.

Preventing pollution is not easy. People do not always agree about the extent of the problem. Sometimes the existence of pollution is obvious, but it is difficult or impossible to prove its harmful effects. For example, the effects of acid rain on trees have yet to be fully understood and the results of increasing amounts of carbon dioxide in the atmosphere may not be known for hundreds of years.

Even when substances are generally recognized as harmful, it may not be a simple matter to prevent their release into the environment because their use may have economic benefits. Thus pesticides and herbicides are still widely used in farming, and radioactive chemicals are still used to provide electricity.

In this book you can read about the main types of pollution and their causes. However, it has been possible to discuss only a few pollution problems and give a brief account of the arguments surrounding them. Some of the issues are very complex and you may want to read other books that deal with different aspects of pollution in greater detail.

CHECK BEFORE YOU EAT

Fish in this water body may be contaminated by mercury or other pollutants.

For safety's sake, you are urged to check your catch – here's how:
1. Identify species
2. Measure length of fish from fork of tail to end of nose
3. Check chart below

If you eat your catch to the maximum recommended for ⬛ or ⬛ you should wait at least six months before doing so again.

If you fish on and off for more than three weeks during the year, and eat your catch, you should consider yourself a long-term consumer.

Children under 15 and women of child-bearing age should eat only. A meal is considered equivalent to 230 grams (8 oz.) Anglers should **not** take fish home for freezing and eating later unless it is from category.

Enjoy your fishing and make your own judgements based on information provided. Additional information is available from Regional and District offices of the Ministries of Environment and Natural Resources.

Good fishing!

Ontario

Category	One Week	Two Weeks	Three Weeks	Long-Term Consumption
	no restrictions	no restrictions	no restrictions	no restrictions
⬛	10 meals or 2.3 kg (5 lbs.) per week	5 meals or 1.3 kg (2.8 lb.) per week	4 meals or 0.95 kg (2.1 lb.) per week	0.226 kg (.5 lb.) per week
⬛	7 meals or 1.54 kg (3.4 lb.) per week	4 meals or 0.86 kg (1.9 lt.) per week	3 meals or 0.63 kg (1.4 lb.) per week	0.136 kg (.3 lb.) per week
🐟	None	None	None	None
🐟	occasional meals only – one or two per week	occasional meals only – one or two per week	occasional meals only – one or two per week	occasional meals only – one or two per month

At Lake Superior in North America a sign warns fishermen that the fish they catch may contain poisonous chemicals.

Many modern chemicals carry some risk of pollution, but their use is usually excused on economic grounds. Is this justified? What level of risk, if any, do you regard as acceptable?

'In many parts of the world, the environment is frequently contaminated with dust and poisonous chemicals resulting from volcanic activity. But because such events are natural, their by-products cannot be considered pollutants.' Do you agree or disagree with this statement?

Air Pollution

The air we breathe consists largely of nitrogen (about 78 per cent) and oxygen (about 21 per cent), together with small quantities of harmless chemicals, such as carbon dioxide, argon and neon. In addition, there are traces of more poisonous chemicals, such as sulphur dioxide, carbon monoxide, nitrogen oxides and ozone, all of which are produced by natural phenomena—volcanoes, lightning and the activity of the sun. Unfortunately, humankind has increased the amounts of these chemicals in the atmosphere and added a number of others. As a consequence, many people, particularly those who live in urban and industrial areas, have to breathe air that contains a number of irritating or poisonous chemicals.

Every day the world's industrial nations pour over 2 million tonnes of pollutants into the atmosphere. Most of these pollutants result from burning fuels and waste materials. Smoke particles, combined with fog and other pollutants, can form a thick, choking smog. The people of London regularly used to suffer such smogs, but the Clean Air Acts of 1956 and 1968, prohibiting the burning of smoky fuels and waste materials, have done much to alleviate this particular problem.

The increasing number of vehicles in our cities is causing the air to become more and more polluted.

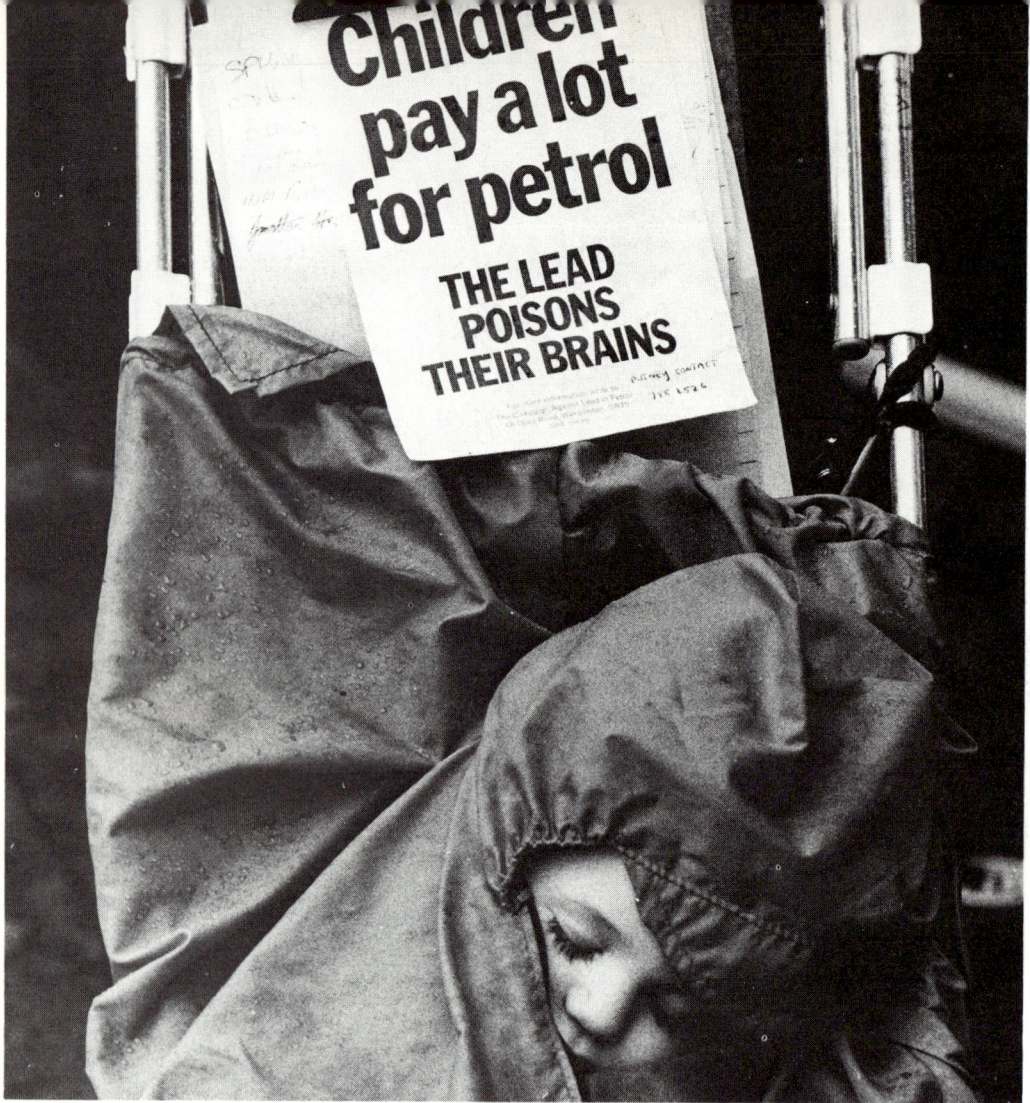

Many people claim that lead pollution from motor vehicle exhausts is even more dangerous than is generally realized.

Pollution by motor vehicle exhausts, on the other hand, has increased. Exhaust fumes contain the highly poisonous gas carbon monoxide as well as unburned hydrocarbons and nitrogen oxides. Some of these hydrocarbons are now known to cause mutations and cancers in animals, and in sunlight they combine with nitrogen oxides and oxygen to form other pollutants, including ozone. These, in turn, may combine with dust or smoke particles to form another type of smog that is a particular hazard in some large cities, notably Los Angeles and Tokyo. In addition, most petrol still contains lead tetraethyl, which is added to make the petrol burn more easily. Car exhausts thus emit lead, a poisonous element known to impede the development of children's brains.

In Czechoslovakia (seen here) and other European countries large numbers of trees are dying, almost certainly because of acid rain.

Burning coal and oil to generate power also causes pollution. Large amounts of the irritant gas sulphur dioxide are produced, together with more nitrogen oxides. In the past it was thought that this form of pollution could be prevented by equipping power stations and industrial complexes with very tall chimneys, so that the gases could be dispersed over a wider area. However, we now know that in the presence of sunlight, sulphur dioxide and nitrogen dioxide combine with other pollutants to form sulphuric, nitric and nitrous acids, which eventually fall as acid rain.

Acid rain eats into limestone and sandstone, and has damaged many stone buildings. It has also affected many lakes, notably in Scandinavia and Canada. Fish and other water life have disappeared from these lakes, partly due to the acidity itself and partly due to poisoning by aluminium, which is leached out of the surrounding soil by the acid. Unfortunately, even if all power stations were to be shut down today, the acid already present in the soil would continue to cause problems for several decades.

Acid rain is also being blamed for the death of many forests. Large areas of forest have already been destroyed in eastern Europe. Trees in most of western Europe also appear to be affected, particularly in West Germany. However, exactly how the trees are being killed has not yet been established.

Burning Amazonian tropical forest to clear land for farming. This practice not only destroys the world's rain forests but also adds to the build-up of carbon dioxide in the air.

Carbon dioxide, the main product of all combustion, may pose another problem. This gas is naturally present in the air and is essential for plant growth. But by burning fuels we have for many years been slowly increasing the amount of carbon dioxide in the atmosphere. A number of scientists believe that this will result in a phenomenon known as the greenhouse effect. The carbon dioxide will trap more heat in the atmosphere and eventually cause a marked rise in the world's temperatures. As yet, this is only a theory— a mathematical model worked out on a computer. It has been suggested that the temperature of the atmosphere might increase by up to 4.5°C by the year 2050. If it does, desert areas like the Sahel would start to receive much needed rain. But at the same time, some productive farmland, as in the American Midwest, would be turned into desert. Eventually, the ice caps would melt, causing the sea to flood many coastal cities. But this process would take place very gradually over thousands of years.

Of more immediate concern is the apparent destruction of the ozone layer. This gas is a poisonous form of oxygen that harms animals and plants at ground level. But high in the atmosphere it forms an essential layer that protects us from the most harmful of the sun's ultraviolet radiation. A recent

American study has shown that, at certain times of the year, the ozone level in one place over Antarctica is only 10 per cent of its normal thickness. It seems possible that the ozone layer is becoming thinner all over the world.

Many scientists believe that the problem is due to chemicals called chlorofluorocarbons (CFCs), which are known to break down ozone. CFCs are widely used in refrigerators and aerosols. In some countries, such as the USA, Canada and Scandinavia, the use of CFCs has now been stopped. Other countries, including Britain, now intend to reduce the production of CFCs, but they still refuse to ban them. If the ozone layer becomes too depleted, the results may be serious. The increased ultraviolet radiation reaching the ground could result in an increase in the incidence of skin cancer, major crop losses and even significant changes in climate around the world.

CFCs, the chemicals used as propellants in many aerosol sprays, are almost certainly causing the destruction of the vital ozone layer.

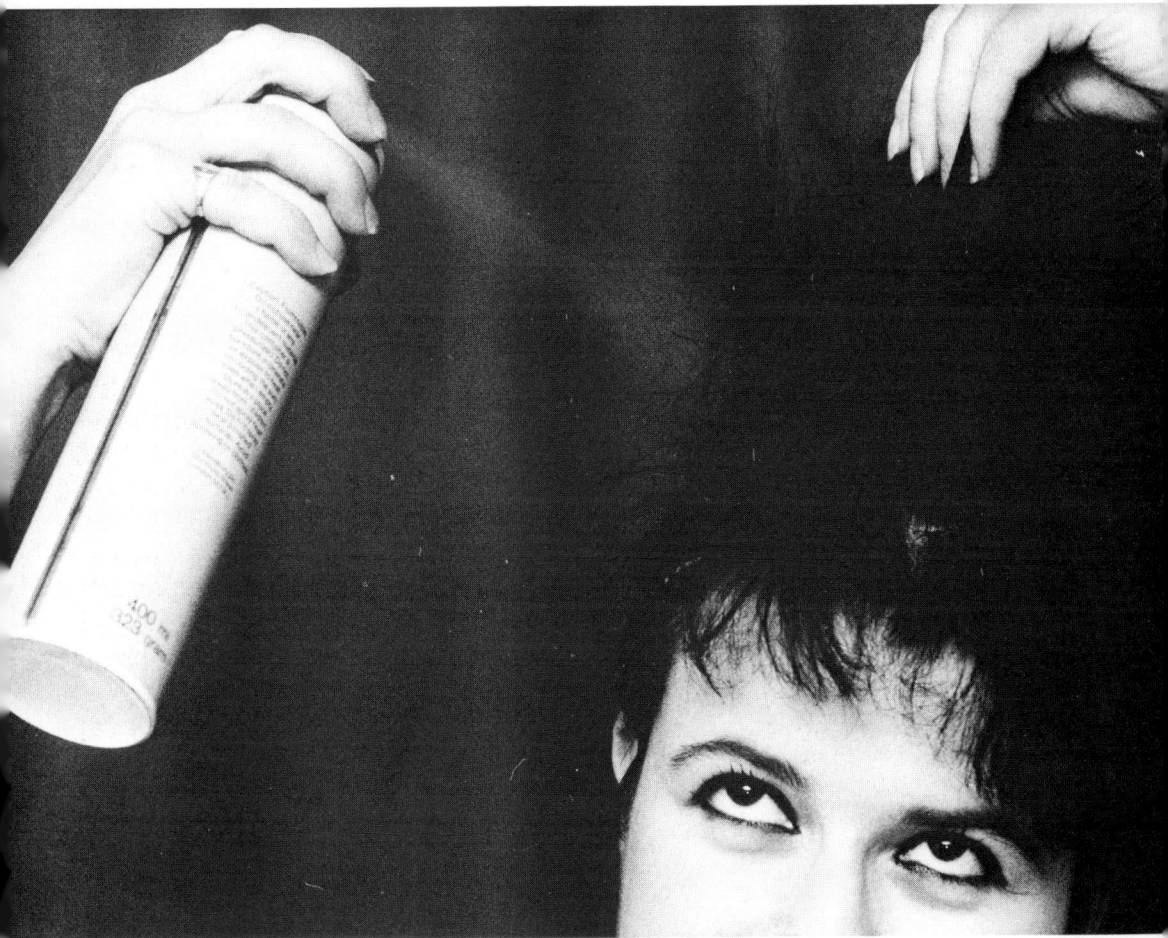

Air pollution can be avoided, or at least reduced. Some countries are beginning to tackle the problem of motor vehicle pollution by introducing lead-free petrol. Most modern cars will run satisfactorily on lead-free petrol, and a car using lead-free petrol can be fitted with a device called a catalytic converter, which removes all the pollutants from the waste gases. Lead-free petrol is more expensive to produce than leaded petrol, so some governments use subsidies to reduce the price. A few car manufacturers are now producing cars with lean-burn engines, which burn fuels more completely.

In a similar way, it is possible to reduce pollution from coal- and oil-fired power stations. Coal and oil can be treated to remove most of the sulphur content. Alternatively, there are new ways of burning coal more efficiently to reduce the level of pollutants in waste gases. It is also possible to use scrubbers to remove pollutants before they reach the outside air. But all these measures cost a great deal of money, and governments and other organizations are often reluctant to invest in what they see as unnecessary precautions. Britain, regarded by many people as one of the worst pollution-producers in Europe, is only now beginning to take action.

Carrying out pollution tests on a car fitted with an exhaust control system. Governments have not yet made such systems compulsory.

Case Study 1:

Dietrich, aged 32

Dietrich teaches science in a school in Freudenstadt, a small town on the edge of the *Schwarzwald*, or Black Forest, in Bavaria. This area relies heavily on the tourist industry and timber for its income. Both Dietrich and his wife are members of the Green Party. They believe passionately that the environment is in urgent need of protection and are particularly concerned about the gloomy prospects for the Black Forest.

Dietrich and his wife spend a lot of time walking in the dense coniferous forest that covers these mountains. 'I have spent all my life in Bavaria and I cannot bear to see the countryside I love destroyed. It is difficult to imagine these mountains without their trees, and yet if something is not done soon, I fear we will lose nearly all of them to the *Waldsterben*, or "forest death", the name we give to this pollution sickness. When you first see the forest, you may think there is no problem. But I can show you many trees with yellowing leaves and weeping twigs. And in some high places, many trees have died. As well as felling mature trees, our foresters are now having to remove young trees that have died or become too damaged. If this is allowed to go on, we will lose so much forest that in five to ten years this area will have no tourists, no income from timber and no drinking water. We will not be able to live here any longer.

'Many people have tried to explain why these things are happening. But whichever idea is correct, it seems clear that some form of pollution must be the cause. Personally, I think that acid rain has to be the main culprit and the problem is certainly getting rapidly worse. So, preventing acid rain must be a top priority. Here in Germany we are doing more than you in Britain, but I do not think that even we are doing enough. All emissions of sulphur dioxide and nitrogen oxides by power stations and industries must be banned completely. Cars, too, must be made to burn fuel cleanly.

'It is probably too late for these measures by themselves to be enough. The acid is already in the soil and it may take tens or hundreds of years for it to be washed out. If we are to save the forests we must repair the damage now by adding lime, magnesium and fertilizers to the soil. This will cost billions of Deutschemarks; but it doesn't matter what it costs, the money must be found.'

A representative of the West German government and a Greenpeace campaigner present an anti acid rain petition to Parliament in 1985.

1 The Black Forest, like most Bavarian forests, is not a truly natural forest—it was planted by people. However, stripped of their trees, the mountains may lose their soil very quickly. Do you agree with Dietrich that the forest must be saved at all costs?

2 Sulphur dioxide and nitrogen oxides are often carried over long distances, with the result that acid rain produced in one country often falls in another. What action do you think should be taken by the countries that produce the pollution?

Discuss the ways in which pollution from cars could be reduced or prevented.

Industrial Pollution

Many of the processes used to turn raw materials into consumer goods produce some form of pollution. When metal ores are mined, for example, large amounts of unwanted materials are mined with them and then dumped on slag heaps. Unfortunately, this often results in pollution, because slag heaps may contain harmful chemicals that are washed out by rainwater.

Processing raw materials may also involve the use or production of potentially lethal chemicals. Although in theory it should be possible to prevent such chemicals from entering the environment, in practice this seems to be almost impossible. Leaks and other accidents do occur, sometimes with catastrophic results. In 1984, over 2,000 people were killed by a massive leak of methyl isocyanate at the Union Carbide factory in Bhopal in India. In 1986, during a fire at the Sandoz chemical plant in Basle, Switzerland, 30 tonnes of agricultural chemicals were accidentally washed into the River Rhine. This caused a 40km long 'wave' of pollution that devastated the wildlife throughout the 800km length of the river.

Firemen trying to control the blaze at the Sandoz chemical factory in Basle, Switzerland. The fire released a cloud of stinking gas and caused severe pollution of the River Rhine.

Modern chemical industry produces some 65,000 different chemicals, most of which sooner or later find their way into the environment. In addition to the pollutants described in the previous chapter, the air people breathe may contain such things as benzene, formaldehyde, silicon tetrafluoride, hydrogen chloride and chlorine, all of which are known to be harmful. Others, such as lead, arsenic, cadmium and mercury, are actually poisonous.

The disposal of waste materials poses an even greater problem. The Western world alone produces about 1 billion tonnes of industrial waste each year. One way of dealing with this waste is to burn it in special incinerators. But this has to be done under carefully controlled conditions, because a number of hazardous chemicals can be destroyed only by being burned at very high temperatures. Even if incineration is carried out correctly, some harmful chemicals are produced. These have to be removed from the waste gases and disposed of, otherwise they only add to the problem of air pollution. Consequently, incineration is often an expensive way to get rid of most waste materials.

Many people believe that we must accept some pollution as result of the manufacture of useful materials like the plastics shown here.

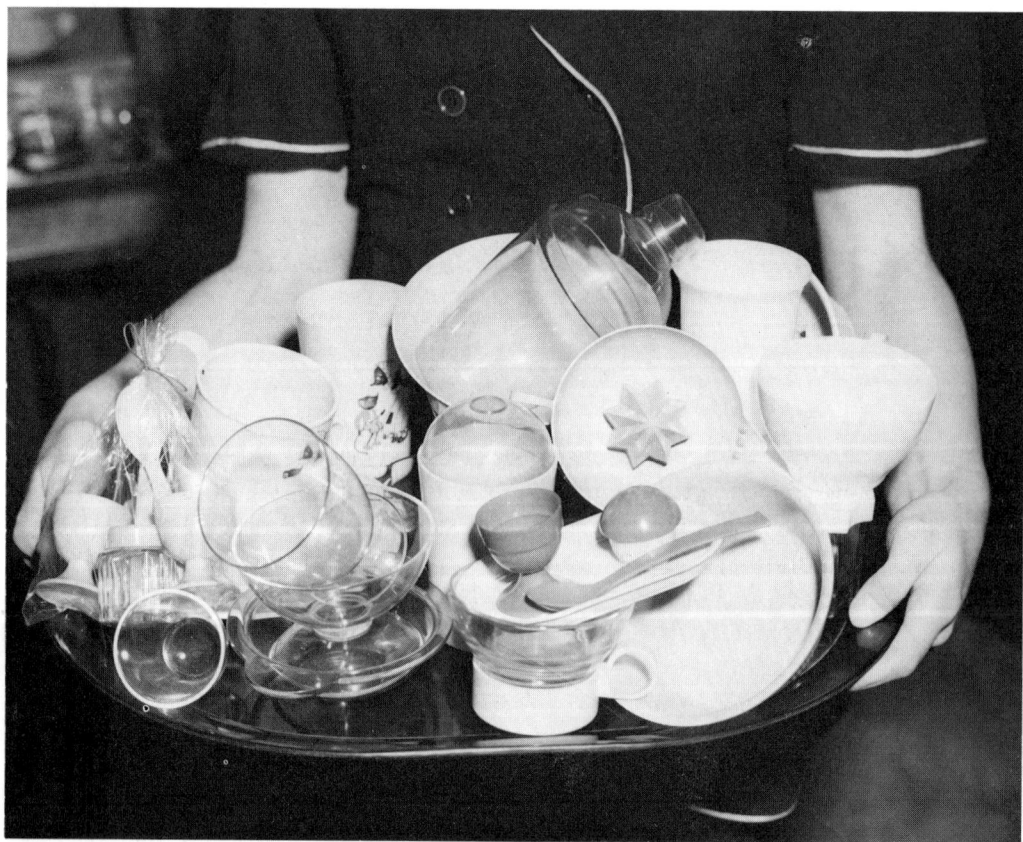

The 2 million cubic metres of rubbish dumped since 1968 in this West German landfill site pollute the air and land around it.

The most commonly used method of waste disposal is landfill. Waste materials are used to fill up holes in the ground, such as pits, quarries, lagoons and old mineshafts, and are later covered with soil. But because most wastes contain harmful chemicals, or produce them as a result of chemical reactions in the waste, landfill disposal itself presents a pollution problem. Harmful chemicals may come up through the soil or be washed out of the site by rain, eventually finding their way into rivers and drinking water. The greatest threat comes from the disposal of poisonous chemicals. It is estimated that between 4 and 12 million tonnes of such hazardous wastes are produced each year in Britain, and many times as much in the USA. Environmentalists claim that only a small proportion, perhaps 10 per cent, of such wastes are disposed of safely.

No one seems to know exactly how many landfill sites there are in Britain, but there may be several hundred. At present, government bodies say that such sites are unlikely to cause problems, but environmentalists maintain that no one can be certain of this. In some countries, such as the USA and France, landfill sites used for toxic chemicals must be lined with clay or a synthetic liner. But in Britain, toxic wastes are generally allowed to seep into the ground. Many people believe that this at least should be prevented, because, as yet, not enough is known about how toxic wastes behave when left underground for a long time. Even lined sites may release hazardous materials, as some chemicals can attack the linings.

Bottle banks are now a familiar sight in many cities and towns. Glass is one of the materials that can be recycled easily.

A workman inspects drums of a hazardous chemical dumped illegally in Rhode Island, USA. Such irresponsible disposal of materials can put lives at risk.

Dumping and incineration both lead to a considerable waste of useful materials. Such waste can be prevented if the materials are recycled. This is most economical where large amounts of one type of material can be collected easily. Metals, paper and glass are particularly suited to recycling and are often recovered in this way. Some plastics can also be recycled, and all organic materials can be composted and eventually returned to the soil. Even some poisonous waste materials can, in a sense, be recycled. The waste is first treated to detoxify the ingredients and the treated chemicals are then blended in huge slurry tanks. The resulting mixture is formed into a non-polluting rock that can be used as a building material. Unfortunately, recycling is less practical for domestic waste, which contains a wide range of materials and sorting this mixture is a very labour-intensive and, hence, expensive task.

Materials that cannot be recycled, particularly the hazardous chemicals produced by industries, must be disposed of safely. But safe methods of disposal are often very expensive and many environmentalists believe that we should stop producing such chemicals altogether.

19

Case Study 2:

Liz, aged 24

On leaving school Liz went to work as a laboratory assistant at a local electroplating company. There she learned a good deal about the potential hazards of chemical wastes. But the company did its best to ensure that all waste chemicals were disposed of according to strict procedures within the law. After about a year, Liz left her job with the electroplating firm for a better paid job with a company that manufactured a range of plastic goods.

'One thing I noticed quite soon was that there were no instructions about handling hazardous chemicals. When I asked about this I was told that this was not really necessary as we didn't produce such chemicals. But then I discovered that a certain amount of trichloroethylene (TCE), a poisonous chemical that can cause cancer and damage to people's livers and kidneys, was being regularly used as a degreasing agent to clean certain bits of machinery.

'Every week, waste TCE was collected into a drum, which was left outside the back of the factory and taken away to a dump after everyone had gone home. I was curious and a bit suspicious,' says Liz. 'So I'm afraid I did some detective work and followed the van that collected the drum. It was carelessly unloaded at the local rubbish dump, creating a dangerous store of TCE.

'Now I had to decide what to do. I knew I might lose my job, but could I stand by and let this go on? Eventually I decided that I had to report it to the County Council.' This she did and the Waste Disposal Officer informed the police. The following week two men were arrested as they unloaded another drum.

The contractor was subsequently prosecuted for illegal dumping of toxic waste, found guilty and fined £1,000. The company denied any knowledge of what had been going on, and nothing could be proved against them. However, they continued to use the services of the same waste disposal contractor, whereas Liz received a redundancy notice shortly afterwards. Liz has since not been able to get a job as a laboratory assistant with any of the local firms and now works as a shop assistant in a greengrocer. 'I'm very bitter at the way I've been treated,' she says. 'I didn't expect to lose my job for acting according to my conscience.'

Thirty years ago the River Thames was severely polluted. Here, an unpleasant foam had accumulated along the bank.

1 Do you think that Liz, as a trusted employee of the plastics manufacturing company, was justified in informing the authorities about the illegal dumping of a relatively small amount of waste?

2 Many of the materials and pieces of equipment that we rely on today, such as plastics and electronic devices, are produced by industries that generate hazardous chemical wastes. Should we tolerate the production of such wastes and look for ways of dealing with them or should we ban them altogether in view of the serious pollution risks?

Discuss the advantages and disadvantages of dealing with waste materials by landfill, incineration and recycling.

Farming and Pollution

Modern farming is an industry, and many people claim that it is just as much to blame for environmental pollution as other industries. Farmers introduce chemicals into the environment deliberately in order to control natural processes. Chemical companies spend vast sums of money persuading farmers to use these chemicals.

Farmers spread manures, animal slurries, sewage sludge and a range of artificial fertilizers on the land in order to make grass, cereals and other crop plants grow more rapidly and vigorously. All these fertilizers contain the nitrogen, phosphorus and potassium necessary for plant growth. But artificial fertilizers do not contain the organic material (from decomposed plant matter) that is vital for maintaining good soil fertility and structure. In areas where these fertilizers are used by themselves on exposed arable land, large amounts of soil are being lost by erosion.

Farmers spray their crops with biocides in order to prevent them being attacked by pests and diseases.

Excess nitrates may be washed off the land into ponds and streams, which become stagnant and lifeless.

Spreading treated sewage sludge on the land might seem to be a good alternative to artificial fertilizers. But although sewage sludge may be rich in organic material, it often contains very little in the way of nitrates, phosphates or potassium compounds; these chemicals are soluble in water and are mostly washed out during the sewage treatment process. If the sludge has come from a treatment plant that deals with industrial as well as domestic effluent, the treated sludge may contain harmful elements, such as lead, cadmium, mercury and fluorine. Sludge taken from cesspits and septic tanks is usually richer in nutrients, but it may also contain a number of potentially dangerous household pollutants.

All manures and fertilizers can cause problems if they are put on the land in excessive amounts. Rainwater may wash a proportion of the nitrates and phosphates out of the soil into rivers and lakes, where they may contribute to a process known as eutrophication. This occurs when nutrient chemicals accumulate in slow-moving or still water and cause a rapid growth of tiny organisms that use up so much oxygen that there is none left for other living things. Fish and invertebrates die and the water becomes almost devoid of life. Streams, rivers and lakes polluted by concentrated animal slurries and silage effluents lose oxygen in a similar way.

Some health food shops now specialize in selling products that have been grown without the help of harmful chemicals.

Nitrates that are washed deeper into the ground eventually get into our drinking water. Some scientists maintain that nitrates are harmless, but others claim that they are harmful to human health. Under certain conditions they can be converted in the body to the more dangerous nitrites. In infants, nitrites may damage the blood circulation to the brain, and in adults, nitrites may cause cancers of the gullet and stomach.

Farmers and growers also use a range of chemical biocides (fungicides, herbicides and pesticides) to destroy unwanted living organisms. Fungicides are sprayed onto crops to kill microscopic moulds, mildews and rusts, which can cause considerable damage. Herbicides are used to kill 'weeds'—that is, plants growing where they are not wanted. As a result, harvesting becomes easier, crop yields are increased and, in the case of cereals, 'contamination' with weed seeds is reduced.

But these advantages are not achieved without some cost to the environment. Many attractive annual 'weeds' are now becoming rare, and just a small amount of spray drift can kill hedgerow plants that cause farmers little or no trouble. Most herbicides are irritants and others are extremely poisonous. Thus any small animals, particularly amphibians and insects unlucky enough to be sprayed may well not survive. Larger animals may also be affected; the widespread use of paraquat (a powerful herbicide that kills most plants) is thought to have led to the reduction in numbers of hares in Britain. Ioxynil, used in over forty different herbicides available in Britain, has been shown to cause birth defects in laboratory animals.

Pesticides are chemicals specifically designed to kill animal life, and are consequently even more dangerous. The most notorious are the organochlorines, such as DDT, dieldrin and eldrin. They remain in the bodies of animals for a long time, and are thus passed along food chains. Small animals containing pesticides are eaten by larger ones, such as badgers, cats and birds of prey. The pesticides accumulate in the bodies of these animals, killing many and causing a general decline in their numbers. The use of DDT and dieldrin is banned in Britain and a number of other countries, but it is still manufactured and exported to developing countries. And despite the ban some farmers and growers still use it.

A sign in Kent warns that the apple trees have been sprayed. Is it genuine, or is it a ruse to stop human pests from picking the apples?

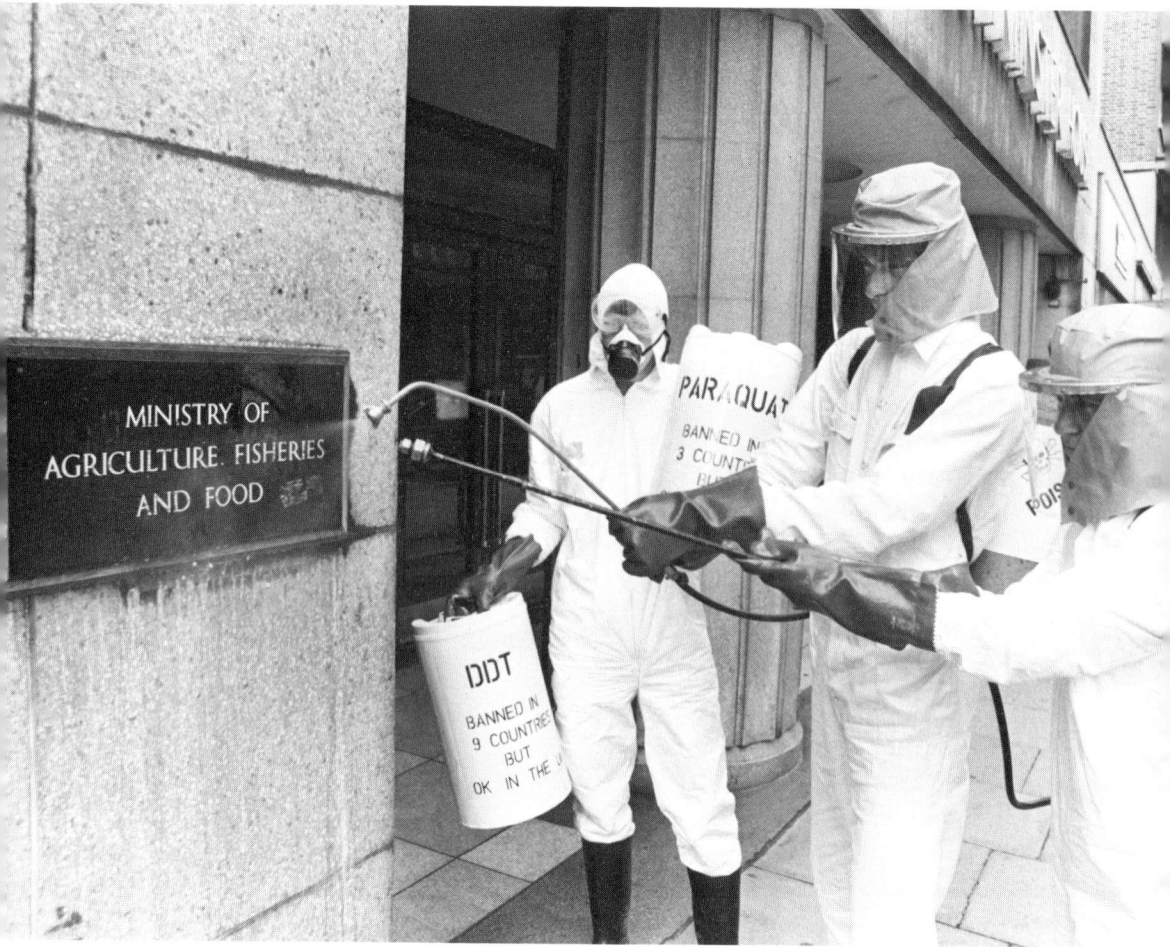

Protesters demonstrating outside the Ministry of Agriculture, Fisheries and Food in London about the use of pesticides in farming.

Organophosphorus pesticides break down more quickly, but are just as lethal. Like all pesticides, they destroy not only the insects they are intended to kill but many other organisms as well, including many that are vital to the good health of the soil. If they are washed into rivers before they break down, they kill fish and other water organisms. Every year there are many cases of people being poisoned by drifting pesticide spray, sometimes blown some distance from the crop being sprayed. Poisoning is particularly common in developing countries, where safety standards are often very poor.

Both pesticides and herbicides are also known to leave residues in the food we eat. People disagree as to whether such residues are harmful. Perhaps this problem will be resolved by the latest pesticides, which are said to be much less toxic to both animals and humans.

Case Study 3:

Brian, aged 48

Brian runs a 100-hectare mixed dairy, beef and arable farm in Dorset, which his father owned before him. He milks a herd of 70 Friesian cows, and has about 50 beef cattle in an intensive unit. He also grows about 50 hectares of cereals (barley and wheat) each year. He works hard himself and employs two farm workers.

Brian is quite vehement in his defence of farming. 'I think it is grossly unfair to say that farmers are a major cause of pollution. On the contrary, many of us do our best to conserve wildlife.

'I know that I and most other farmers use chemicals. But I have to in order to get a decent income from the land I own. Anyway, let's just look at the chemicals I use. For instance, I have to use fertilizers or I just don't get enough hay and silage off my fields to feed my animals. Nor do I get an economic yield from my crops.

'I know that some of the fertilizer I put on is washed away, but I reckon I lose only a little. I don't put all my fertilizer on in one go, and if I time it right, most of it is taken up by the grass—that takes only three days. In any case the runoff from my rather clayey ground is probably less of a problem than it is on farms with sandy or limestone soils.

'Then there's what they call biocides. Again, if I didn't use them, I wouldn't make enough profit on my crops. I know that some people are saying that fungicides and herbicides harm animals and people, but they haven't managed to prove it.

'Pesticides, I agree, are more of a problem. One very real difficulty is that a lot of pests are becoming resistant to them—we're actually creating so-called super bugs. Some pesticides are, I admit, pretty lethal. But I don't use those and I don't think anyone should. They shouldn't be used anywhere in the world, but the more dangerous ones are cheaper and most of the farmers in developing countries can't afford to buy expensive chemicals. So, what should they use instead?

'Maybe such chemicals should be banned. But everyone would have to stop using them, so that we are all left in the same position. If we all go 'organic', then people will have to pay more for their food. But in any case, I'm not convinced that using so-called organic chemicals won't lead to many of the same problems we have now.'

Not all farm chemicals are pollutants. Here a farmer is spreading lime in order to decrease the acidity of the soil.

1 Do you think that Brian has a right to do what he likes on his own land? If not, why not, and what limits would you impose on him, and farmers like him?

2 Which, if any, of these views do you agree with?
   a) All artificial pesticides should be banned.
   b) All pesticides, including organic pesticides, should be banned.
   c) The most harmful pesticides should be banned, but we should continue to use the less poisonous ones.

Discuss the view that it should be illegal to release into the environment chemicals whose long-term effects are not fully understood.

Water Pollution

The only unpolluted natural water in the modern world is the pure water obtained by melting ice laid down in glaciers thousands of years ago, before humans started polluting the earth. All other water is, to some degree, polluted. In many cases, of course, pollution levels are so low that they are relatively unimportant. But all too often water pollution destroys wildlife.

Throughout the world, industries produce a variety of liquid and solid wastes that are allowed to pollute water courses. In many countries, there are rivers and lakes so polluted that they are totally devoid of any life. In Britain, a law passed in 1961 made it illegal to release untreated industrial effluents into waterways, and some rivers, such as the River Thames, are a great deal cleaner than they were thirty years ago. But many other British

In 1971 the River Lys in France was severely polluted when detergent was dumped in the water.

rivers and waterways still carry the froth that indicates severe industrial pollution. Some streams are contaminated by the effluent that leaks from badly maintained cesspits and septic tanks. In addition, rivers may contain farming chemicals washed off the land and chemicals released from sewage treatment plants. Among these are phosphates from household detergents, which in some places are the main cause of eutrophication of rivers and lakes (see page 23). Sometimes water pollution is due to chemicals released when land is disturbed, for instance, when moorland is ploughed, or the foundations of new buildings or motorways are excavated.

The River Seine in France is visibly polluted. Stinking dead fish float in an oily scum on the surface.

We regard water from the kitchen tap as safe to drink. But some people claim that it may not be as safe as we think.

Few natural sources of water are considered safe to drink. Much of the water delivered to our homes is taken from rivers and processed by water treatment plants. There, all the solid matter is removed and chlorine is added to kill bacteria and other disease-causing organisms. However, there are a number of chemicals that remain in the water after it is treated in this way, some of which are known to be harmful. Examples include benzene, chloroform and trichloroethylene. Some scientists maintain that the quantities of these chemicals are so small that their presence is not a problem. But environmentalists claim that even treated drinking water may well be unsafe to drink.

Sewage sludge that is not spread on the land (see page 22) is sometimes held in deep 'ponds', from where chemicals may well seep out into groundwater. Another way of getting rid of it is to dump it in the sea; this method is also used to dispose of a great deal of industrial waste, including large quantities of mine wastes. In some places high concentrations of waste chemicals cause a great deal of damage to communities of sea organisms and, again, the long-term effects of these substances are not always known. A number of them build up in marine food chains, and many edible fish and shellfish now contain poisons, including DDT, mercury and lead.

In the coastal areas of many countries, sewage is not even treated before being pumped into the sea, often very close to popular bathing beaches. This is not only very unpleasant but also extremely hazardous to human health. Despite attempts by the European Economic Community (EEC) to control such pollution, Britain still has many beaches polluted by sewage. Even worse are the contaminated waters found around the Mediterranean Sea, where there are no tides and few currents.

Oil pollution is another common hazard in the world's seas. At one end of the scale there are unsightly lumps of tar caused by small spillages and discharges from passing ships. Although these are unpleasant, particularly when washed onto beaches, they do not pose too much of a threat to wildlife. On the other hand, major oil slicks can devastate large areas. Hundreds or thousands of seabirds may be killed when their feathers become saturated with oil. In shallow water, shellfish and other bottom-dwellers may be suffo-cated—oil pollution does much more than spoil attractive beaches.

In many coastal places untreated sewage is discharged into the sea. Often tides and currents bring it back to the shore.

Oil pollution can have a devastating effect on birds. Here, on the Island of Fehmarn in the Baltic Sea, 25 oil-covered ducks were washed ashore on a beach that is used as a nature reserve.

Oil slicks are treated first with detergents to break them up. These detergents are not toxic to most sea life, but the globules of oil they produce may be swallowed by fish. Other ways of removing oil from the sea include the use of floating booms, skimmers and special ropes, but these can be used effectively only on relatively small slicks. Large slicks from major tanker accidents will continue to cause widespread devastation. Fortunately, such incidents are becoming less frequent.

1 *What do you think we as individuals can do to help prevent water being polluted?*

2 *Some industries continue to pollute our rivers, in spite of the fact that they can be prosecuted and fined up to £2,000 (most fines are less than £1,000). Can you think of any ways of further discouraging such pollution?*

Discuss the arguments for and against the disposal of waste in the world's oceans.

Radioactivity

Radioactivity is, in many ways, very useful, but it can also be very harmful. Unlike other forms of pollution, it cannot be detected by sight or smell, and its effects may be difficult to see. As a result, radioactive materials are probably the most feared of all modern pollutants.

Radioactive elements, or radioisotopes, produce radiation that harms living organisms by breaking up atoms in living tissues. Radioactive substances are all about us. A number occur quite naturally in the ground; examples include uranium, radium, radon, polonium and two radioactive forms of lead. In addition, a range of artificial radioisotopes now exists. Some of these

At nuclear power stations stringent safety measures must be taken to make sure that workers are not exposed to unsafe levels of radiation.

Many people and animals have suffered from the high level radiation
released when the nuclear reactor at Chernobyl, USSR, exploded in 1986.

are created by bombarding non-radioactive elements with beams of subatomic particles. Other radioisotopes are created by similar processes that occur inside nuclear reactors.

Due to the presence of natural radioisotopes we are subjected to a small amount of background radiation all the time. This does us little or no harm, as our bodies can tolerate a certain amount of radiation. However, higher concentrations of radioactive chemicals are more dangerous. Even moderate levels of radiation may result in leukaemia and other types of cancer, and very high levels cause skin burns, radiation sickness and death.

Very high concentrations of radioisotopes are found in nuclear reactors. But like all dangerous substances, radioisotopes pose no pollution threat if they can be adequately contained. The core of a nuclear reactor is therefore encased in a thick layer of shielding material and every effort is made to prevent the escape of any radioactive matter. There are controls designed to shut down the reactor in emergencies, and the people who work there are constantly monitored to ensure that they are not subjected to too much radiation.

Those people in favour of using nuclear power maintain that, generally speaking, safety precautions are adequate. Opponents of the nuclear industry point to the fact that over the years there have been a number of accidents involving radioactive materials at nuclear power stations. In 1979, for example, a cooling system failed at the Three Mile Island pressurized water reactor in Pennsylvania, USA. As a result, a great deal of radioactive water was released and the uranium nuclear fuel came close to melting. The resulting explosion would have produced a huge cloud of radioactive dust that would have contaminated a very large area.

More recently, in 1986, an accident occurred at the notorious Chernobyl reactor in the USSR. A combination of design faults and human stupidity produced an explosion that released a cloud of radioactive dust. Winds carried this dust across many parts of Europe and Asia, and in places where rain fell, the ground became contaminated with radioisotopes. Radioactive caesium then contaminated the meat of grazing animals, particularly sheep and reindeer, and may continue to cause problems for several years. At the same time, many people were subjected to fairly high levels of radiation and this will almost certainly cause cancer in some of them. The accident at Chernobyl has caused many people to question the safety of all nuclear reactors, wherever they may be. Supporters of the nuclear industry maintain that lessons have been learned and such an accident cannot happen again.

Even if nuclear power stations can be made completely safe, the problem of finding somewhere to dispose of waste is still not solved. Spent nuclear fuel has to be reprocessed and this generates radioactive waste. In Britain the nuclear reprocessing plant at Sellafield has achieved some notoriety during the last few years. To begin with, there is a constant deliberate discharge of some radioactive materials into the Irish Sea, including a form of plutonium that has a half-life of 24,400 years. As a result, local beaches

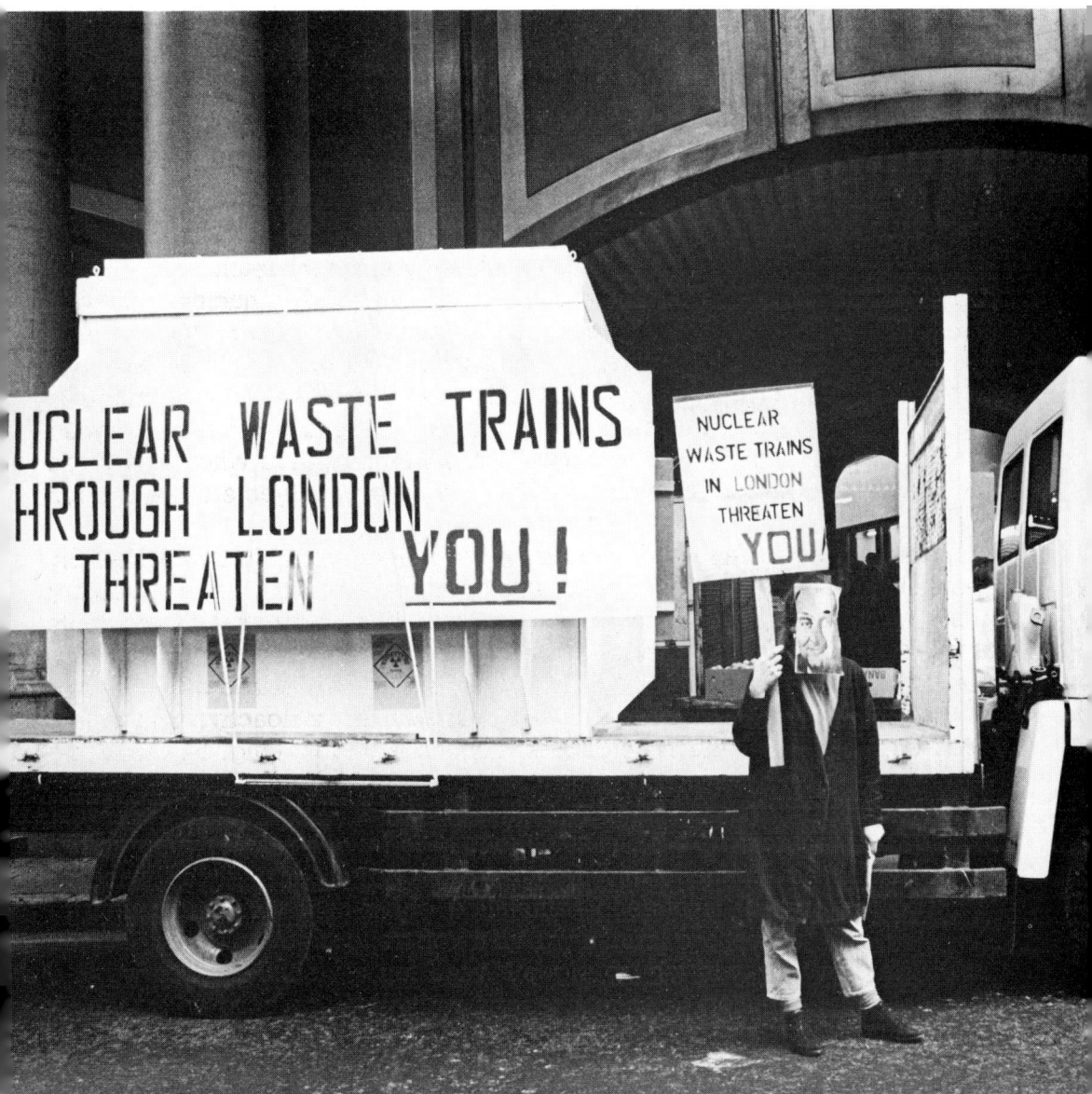

Friends of the Earth campaigners protest about the transport of nuclear waste containers through London. The nuclear power industry has had difficulty in finding an acceptable way to dispose of waste matter.

have been contaminated. Many people regard this as unacceptable, although nuclear scientists maintain there is no danger. Furthermore, on a number of occasions radioactive chemicals have leaked into the air and the surrounding soil. These leaks are suspected of having caused an increase in the number of cases of leukaemia among local people.

The nuclear waste reprocessing plant at Sellafield is considered by many to release unacceptable amounts of radioactive materials.

The highly radioactive waste (high-level waste) produced during the reprocessing of spent nuclear fuel must be stored safely for thousands of years. Both nuclear reactors and reprocessing plants also produce medium-level waste. In addition, radioisotopes are used in medicine, research and in a number of industries, all of which produce huge amounts of low-level waste. Since 1949 a great deal of low-level and medium-level waste has been encased in concrete and dumped on the ocean floor. However, no one knows for certain what the long-term consequences of this will be, particularly for the marine life in these areas. Another way of getting rid of this waste is to bury it in the ground, but this has recently become very unpopular and finding suitable sites is increasingly difficult. Many people now favour the idea of burying all nuclear waste, including high-level waste, in specially prepared underground repositories, possibly under the sea bed. Opponents of this idea point out that it is very difficult to predict what will happen to such repositories over thousands of years.

Nuclear reactors are not the only potential source of radioactive pollution. An exploding nuclear weapon not only produces a devastating blast but also a whole range of dangerous isotopes. Any large-scale use of such weapons in a war would leave vast areas of the world virtually uninhabitable. So the use of nuclear weapons is regarded by some people as the ultimate form of pollution.

CND, the Campaign for Nuclear Disarmament, organizes many protests against both nuclear weapons and nuclear power.

Case Study 4:

Malcolm, aged 46

Malcolm graduated as a physicist twenty-two years ago. After a period as a research scientist, he joined the nuclear power industry and now works at a nuclear power station in England.

Malcolm believes that nuclear power is necessary. 'We should not rely on coal and oil to supply us with power. The world's oil may run out even in my lifetime and we need the chemicals that can be extracted from it. So it is far too valuable to burn. Coal supplies will last a lot longer, I know, but future generations are not going to thank us for burning it all now. And in any case, I agree with the politicians who say that we should not rely on only one industry to supply us with power; it makes that industry, and its unions, too powerful.

'I agree that we should try to make use of wind power and tidal power. Perhaps we should also do some more research into alternative methods of generating power. But don't forget that all these methods of power production are going to have some effect on the environment. Besides, they are not likely to produce very much of the power we are going to need in the future.'

Malcolm also believes that nuclear power is basically clean and safe, compared with other methods of power generation. 'Just look at the air pollution produced by coal-fired power stations. It can be prevented, I know, but remember that every tonne of sulphur you remove from the waste gases produces 4 tonnes of sulphurized lime-stone in the "scrubber". That has to be disposed of, too.

'Of course, there are some risks in using nuclear power, and there have been accidents. But what industry does not have some accidents? Cars kill thousands every year and yet few people say that we must do without them. They should, of course, be made as safe as possible, and that is what we are trying to do in the nuclear industry. An accident like the one at Chernobyl cannot happen here. Our power stations are much more safely built—the Chernobyl operators actually switched off the safety systems!

'The problem of nuclear waste will eventually be solved. Personally, I think the best way of dealing with it is to excavate stores deep underground. We know of rock formations that have remained undisturbed for tens of thousands of years, so rock movement should not be a problem.'

The coal-fired Fiddlers Ferry power station in Lancashire. If we abandon
nuclear energy, we will have to rely on such power stations to produce
most of our electricity.

1   To what extent do you agree with Malcolm about the need for
    nuclear power stations?

2   Do you agree or disagree that the risks of using nuclear power
    are justified?

'High-level radioactive waste that will remain dangerous for many
thousands of years is too dangerous to store in any way. We should
therefore gradually close down all nuclear power installations and
increase the amount of power generated by other means.' Discuss
this view.

Pollution and Society

The solutions to the problems of pollution are not likely to be easy, largely because people's views and attitudes vary so widely. At one extreme are those who hold the view that the modern world needs the machines, chemicals and materials that are currently produced and that some pollution is an inevitable result of their manufacture and use. At the other extreme are those who believe that no pollutants should be released into the environment and that the most harmful substances should not even be created. They argue that even if pollutants cannot be proved to cause major damage, the potential risk to the environment is too great.

The greatest progress in cleaning up the environment has been due to changes in the law. However, most governments are by nature very cautious and progress is therefore very slow. It is usually necessary to prove conclusively that serious harm is being done before protective measures are introduced. But it is probably the opinion of the general public that is most effective

Despite laws, fines and even nearby public tips, some people dump rubbish illegally—without any consideration for others.

*In 1979 a fishing match was organized on the River Thames to demonstrate
how clean the river had become.*

in forcing governments to take action. Public opinion is influenced by television, newspapers, books and magazines, as well as pressure groups, such as Friends of the Earth, Greenpeace, the Green Party, the World Wildlife Fund and many others.

The manufacturing and chemical industries are often regarded as the worst polluters. However, many of these industries are now beginning to clean up some of their pollution and undertake research into environmental problems. This is partly because they have been compelled to by changes in the law, and partly because they are responding to changes in public opinion. Our rivers are much cleaner than they used to be, the latest pesticides are much less harmful than their predecessors, and one chemical company has now developed a biodegradable plastic.

But if public opinion is to be a major factor in the control of pollution, perhaps we should examine our own attitudes and behaviour more closely. Advertising works only if we buy the products advertised; so perhaps we should be more critical about what we buy. Most of us disapprove of pollution, but what action are we actually prepared to take? Perhaps we should be more reluctant to use such things as leaded petrol, aerosols with CFC propellants, and detergents that contain phosphates. Can we justify protesting about acid rain and nuclear power, while we make our own contributions to environmental pollution?

To take a simple example, which of us is not guilty of discarding a piece of litter at some time? Just examine any street or roadside layby in Britain to see the results of the careless disposal of litter. In some cases people dump large amounts of rubbish in odd corners of our cities and give someone else the expense and trouble of clearing it up. The practice is known as fly-tipping and the fact that it is illegal seems to make no difference.

Pollution is a problem that cannot be treated effectively in isolation. It is inevitably linked with other world issues, such as the use of land and resources, energy production, world health and environmental conservation. Solutions may require the consent of different nations, each one of which includes people of widely differing views, so it is also a matter of international politics. Some environmentalists believe that the world's major problems, including that of pollution, will be solved only by completely changing the current economic and political order. Others believe that human nature will prevent any such change, and besides, the new order might not be any better. What do you think?

The General Assembly of the United Nations. International cooperation will be needed to solve the world's pollution problems.

Ultimately we determine the nature of our environment—if we treat it like a rubbish tip, that is what it will become.

1 Many people, while recognizing that some waste materials, such as domestic rubbish and nuclear waste, must be placed in dumps, object to having such dumps located near them—the NIMBY (Not In My Back Yard) syndrome. Who ought to be involved in decisions about where to put waste?

2 Do you think that the large amounts of litter that can be found in Britain indicates a society that cares little about pollution?

'Modern society inevitably creates waste. We cannot stop polluting the world unless we all change the way we live.' Discuss this opinion.

Glossary

Acid rain The transfer of acid-forming pollutants, mainly sulphur dioxide and nitrogen oxides, from the air to the ground in rain, snow, hail, mist or dust.

Carbon dioxide A gas formed from the chemical combination of carbon and oxygen. Each molecule contains one carbon atom and two oxygen atoms. It is formed when fuels are burned and is the gas breathed out by all animals. Plants need carbon dioxide to build up new plant material.

Carbon monoxide A poisonous gas formed from the chemical combination of carbon and oxygen. Its molecules contain one carbon atom and only one atom of oxygen. It is generally formed as a result of the incomplete burning of a fuel.

Chlorofluorocarbon (CFC) A chemical whose molecules contain carbon atoms combined with both chlorine and fluorine atoms. CFCs do not break down easily in the air. They eventually find their way to the ozone layer. There they release chlorine, which causes ozone to break down into ordinary oxygen.

Environment All the conditions that exist around one or more living organisms. The natural environment includes such things as temperature, sunlight, rainfall, air, soil and other living things.

Fertilizer Any material added to soil in order to increase its ability to grow plants.

Fossil fuel A fuel formed from the remains of animals or plants that lived millions of years ago. The main fossil fuels are coal, oil and natural gas.

Greenhouse effect The (theoretical) process where gradually increasing amounts of carbon dioxide in the atmosphere will cause it to warm up.

Heat rays from the sun are absorbed by the gases in the atmosphere and by the solid and liquid materials on the earth's surface. All these materials then re-emit heat, but the carbon dioxide in the atmosphere acts like the glass of a greenhouse and prevents some of this heat from escaping.

Half-life The time taken for half of the atoms present in a piece of radioactive material to decay into atoms of another element.

Hydrocarbon A chemical whose molecules are made up only of carbon and hydrogen atoms. Such chemicals are found in crude oil and some of its products, such as petrol.

Isotope Any one of two or more forms of the same element. Hydrogen, for example, has three isotopes—hydrogen (hydrogen-1), deuterium (hydrogen-2) and tritium (hydrogen-3).

Leukaemia A cancer-like disease of certain cells in the blood.

Nitrogen oxides Chemicals that consist chemically of nitrogen combined with varying amounts of oxygen. They are produced by the burning of fossil fuels, including petrol.

Organic 1: (In chemistry) A chemical whose molecules are based on carbon atoms. 2: (In farming and gardening) A system of food production that does not use any synthetic chemicals, relying instead on natural products for maintaining the productivity of the soil and keeping down pests.

Radioisotope A radioactive isotope.

Silage effluent Nitrogen-containing fluid that is sometimes produced during the process of fermenting grass into the cattle fodder known as silage.

Slag Waste rock produced during mining for metals or coal.

Sulphur dioxide A gas that consists chemically of a combination of sulphur and oxygen. It is often formed when fossil fuels are burned.

Toxic Poisonous.

Ultraviolet radiation Invisible radiation of the same type as light rays and radio waves, but with wavelengths slightly shorter than those of visible light. The strong ultraviolet radiation produced by the sun can damage living tissue.

Further Reading

Acid Rain by Phillip Neal (Dryad Press, 1985)

Acid Rain by Steve Elsworth (Pluto Press, 1984)

Air Ecology by Jennifer Cochrane (Wayland, 1987)

Blueprint for a Green Planet by John Seymour and Herbert Girardet (Dorling Kindersley, 1987)

Focus on Alternative Energy by Paul McClory (Wayland, 1985)

Focus on Coal by Theodore Rowland-Entwistle (Wayland, 1987)

Focus on Oil by Mark Lambert (Wayland, 1986)

Focus on Plastics by Mark Lambert (Wayland, 1987)

Green Britain or Industrial Wasteland, edited by Edward Goldsmith and Nicholas Hildyard (Polity Press, 1986)

Land Ecology by Jennifer Cochrane (Wayland, 1987)

Pollution by Michael J. Gittins (National Society for Clean Air, 1983)

Silent Spring by Rachel Carson (Penguin, 1982)

The Breathing Planet, edited by John Gribben (New Scientist Guides, 1987)

The Countryside Under Threat by L. Bolwell and C. Lines (Wayland, 1987)

The Energy Crisis by Michael Gibson (Wayland, 1987)

The Environment by Adam Markham (Wayland, 1988)

The Future for the Environment by Mark Lambert (Wayland, 1986)

The Gaia Atlas of Planet Management, edited by Norman Myers (Good Books, 1985)

The Green Alternative, edited by Peter Bunyard and Fern Morgan-Grenville (Methuen, 1987)

Water Ecology by Jennifer Cochrane (Wayland, 1987)

Acknowledgements

The publishers would like to thank the following for providing the illustrations in this book: Camera Press 10, 21, 30, 33, 35, 44; Greenpeace Media 9 (Zindler); Hutchison 6; Frank Lane *front cover*, 22, 23 (David Grewcock), 28 (R. P. Lawrence), 41 (W. Broadhurst); Bürgerinitiative Gegen Giftmüll 17 (Peter Kistler); Photo Co-op 18 (Crispin Hughes), 32 (Corry Bevington), 34 (Sarah Wyld), 37 (Janis Austin), 42 (Crispin Hughes); Popperfoto 4, 5, 7, 15, 29, 38, 39, 43; Mark Power 11, 24, 31, 45; Topham 8, 12, 14, 16, 19, 25, 26.

Index

accidents causing pollution
  Basle 15
  Bhopal 4, 15
  Chernobyl 4, 36, 40
  Three Mile Island 36
acid rain 5, 9, 13, 43
animal slurry 22–3

biodegradable plastic 43
Black Forest 13–14

cancer 8, 11, 24, 36–7
carbon dioxide 5, 7, 10
carbon monoxide 7, 8
catalytic converters 12
chemicals 4–6, 22, 27, 42
  farming 30
  hazardous 15–21
  organic 27
  radioactive 5, 33
chlorofluorocarbons 11, 43
Clean Air Acts 7
conservation 44
crop spraying 5, 24, 26

DDT 25, 31
detergents 33, 43
drinking water 17, 24, 31

environmentalists 4, 12, 18–19
eutrophication 23, 30

fertilizers 13, 22–3, 27
fungicides 24

greenhouse effect 10

herbicides 5, 24, 26
hydrocarbons 8

incinerators 16, 19, 21

landfill 17–18, 21
lead 8, 16, 23, 31, 34
lead-free petrol 12
litter 44–5

manure 22
Mediterranean Sea 32

nitrates 23–4
nitrogen oxides 7–9, 14
nuclear power 36, 38–40, 43
nuclear weapons 39

oil 9, 46
oil slicks 32–3
ozone 7–8, 10–11

pesticides 5, 24–8, 43
phosphates 23, 30, 43
power stations 9, 12–13, 40

radiation 34, 36
recycling 19, 21
rivers 17, 29–30, 43

Sellafield 36
sewage 4, 22–3, 31–2
slag heaps 15
smog 7–8
sulphur dioxide 7, 9, 13–14

ultraviolet radiation 10

Waste Disposal Officer 20
waste materials 4, 17
  chemical 20, 21
  domestic 19, 44
  industrial 16, 31
  poisonous 19
wildlife 15, 27, 29